I0008575

Programming for Beginners:

Fundamental Basics of C++, Java and Python

Start programming right now!

By Mark Smart

Table of Contents

Disclaimer

While all attempts have been made to verify the information provided in this book, the author does assume any responsibility for errors, omissions, or contrary interpretations of the subject matter contained within. The information provided in this book is for educational and entertainment purposes only. The reader is responsible for his or her own actions and the author does not accept any responsibilities for any liabilities or damages, real or perceived, resulting from the use of this information.

The trademarks that are used are without any consent, and the publication of the trademark is without permission or backing by the trademark owner. All trademarks and brands within this book are for clarifying purposes only and are the owned by the owners themselves, not affiliated with this document. **

Introduction

Computer program is the art of instructing a computer to do something. Who on earth won't desire to do this? With knowledge in programming, you can create your own program and accomplish too much. C++, Java and Python are some of the popular programming languages in the market. These programming languages are also in high demand because of their high degree of flexibility. One can also achieve a lot with these programming languages. The languages support the use of object-oriented features such as classes and objects, which make it easy for one to create and run programs. This book guides you on how to program in these programming languages even if you are a beginner.

Chapter 1- C++

C++ is the best language for those who need to communicate to machines. It is an object oriented programming language which can be used for developing anything including video games, desktop applications and system design.

You can also use C++ to create high-performance applications such as operating systems and web servers, and game engines which currently in use.

Getting Started

There are several environments online on which you can execute your C++ programs for free. However, it is good for you to know how to setup your own environment on your local computer.

For you to set up the environment locally, you should have a Text Editor and the C++ compiler. Some of the editors which you can use include Windows Notepad, Brief, Epsilon, EMACS, OS Edit command and vim

.

Once you have written your program on the editor, it will form the source file, and this file should be named with a ".cpp", ".cp" or ".c" extension. Ensure that your computer has a text editor before we can get started.

The C++ compiler will be used for transforming/compiling the source code (program) which you have written into a form which the computer can execute.

Now that you have a text editor on your computer, it is time for you to set up the C++ compiler by installing it. If you are using a distribution of Linux operating system, run the following command on the terminal to check whether the C++ compiler has been installed:

$ g++ -v

If it is readily installed, you will get the gcc (Gnu C compiler) version. If not, then you will have to install it.

For Mac OS X users, just download the XCode development environment from the web site for Apple and then install it.

For the case of Windows users, you will have to download and install the MinGW.

C++ Syntax

A C++ program can be seen as a combination of objects which communicate via invocation of methods belonging to the different objects. Let us discuss the meaning of some of the terms used in C++:

1. Object- an object should have state and behavior. It represents an instance of a class.

2. Class- this is a blueprint or a template describing the states/behaviors which the objects of its type should support.

3. Method- a method is simply a behavior. A single class can have multiple methods which can be used for manipulation of both data and behavior.

4. Instance variables- each object in C++ is associated with some instance variables, each being unique.

Hello world Example

Let us write our first program in C++, this should print "Hello world".

Open your favorite text editor and write the following code in it:

#include <iostream>

```
using namespace std;
// the execution of the program begins at main()
int main()
{
    cout << "Hello world"; // to print Hello World
    return 0;
}
```

That is the program! Very simple! Maybe you expected the whole page to be filled. No.

The C++ programming language comes with several headers and each of these headers has information which is useful to the program. In the above program, we are using the header "<iostream>". The use of the line "using namespace std" tells the C++ compiler to make use of the std namespace. C++ introduced namespaces recently.

The next line of code begins with "//". The two forward slashes are used to tell the C++ compiler that we are writing a comment, and that it should not bother to execute it, but it should skip and proceed to the next line of code. The symbol // denotes that it is a single-line comment.

The "int main()" line denotes where the execution of our program will begin. The use of ()" brackets shows that we have created a function. Functions are written with brackets at the end as shown above.

The "cout<<"Hello world"; line will print the message "Hello world" on the screen. The "cout" stands for "console output", meaning that it will output some value or words on the console.

You can now save the above program, giving it the name "hello.cpp". Open the command prompt then navigate to the directory you have saved your file. You can then type the following on this command prompt:

g++ hello.cpp

The above command will work to compile your source code. Note that if there are errors in your program, they are detected during compile time. If your program has no errors, then an "a.out" file will be created, which is an executable file and you will be taken to the next line.

You can then type "./a.out" on the terminal so as to run/execute the program. You will see the text "Hello world" printed on the screen. The sequence of steps should be as follows:

$ g++ hello.cpp

$ ./a.out

You will then get the following output on the console:

Hello world

Also, you have to ensure that the g++ has been added to the path variable in addition to having navigated to the directory in which you have stored the C++ file.

Blocks and Semicolons

In C++, the semicolon(;) operator is used for terminating statements. When a semicolon has been added, it shows that a logical entity has ended. The following statements demonstrate this:

p = q;

q = q+1;

add(p, q);

A block represents a collection of logical statements which are enclosed within curly braces {}. The following example demonstrated this:

```
{
    cout << "Hello world"; // to print Hello World
    return 0;
}
```

Note that in C++, the end of line does not mean that it has terminated, meaning the point on a line a statement is added is not of importance. Consider the following example:

The code:

```
p = q;
q = q+1;
add(p, q);
```

Is just the same as **p = q; q = q+1; add(p, q);**

Once the C++ compiler finds the semicolon (;) operator, then it will know that the statement has just ended. That is it!

C++ Comments

In C++ and any other programming language, comments are used for explanation purpose so that anyone reading the code can easily understand it.

In C++, both single-line and multi-line comments are supported. The C++ compiler will ignore any characters written inside your comment.

In C++, comments begin with "/*" and they end with "*/". Consider the example given below:

/* This is an example of a comment */

/* It is possible for C++ comments to

 * span multiple lines

 */

A single line comment is denoted by use of "//" symbol and the comment will extend to the end of the line.

That sounds good!

C++ Variables

In our "Hello world" example, you knew how to write a program which will print text on the screen.

The definition of a variable involves telling the C++ compiler where and the amount of storage space that should be created for the variable. A variable name should only have letters, digits and underscore character. However, the variable name has to begin with either a letter or the underscore character. If the name begins with a digit or any other special character other than the underscore, then it will be invalid. I am sure this sounds funny to you, but you will understand it shortly!

Variable Types

The following are some of the variable types which are supported in C++:

1. bool- this will store either a true or false value.

2. char- this is an int type, and a single octet

3. int- this forms the most natural size for an integer for machine

4. float- this is some single-precision value

5. double- some double-precision floating point value

6. void- this means that the value is not present

Despite the presence of all the above types of variables, it is also possible for one to define some other types of variables. These include Enumeration, Array, Pointer, Reference, Classes and Data structures.

The definition of variables in C++ takes the following syntax:

type variable_list;

Also, it will be good for you to be aware that C++ is case sensitive, meaning that you have to be keen when writing the names as you may experience difficulties due to use of lowercase and uppercase letters anyhow. Consider the following examples:

int salary;
int Salary;

In the above example, we have defined two variables and they are of an integer data type. This is designated by use of the "int" keyword, which stands for an "integer".

In the first definition of the variable, we have named the variable "salary", with the letter "s" being written in lowercase. In the second example, the "S" is in uppercase, and this makes the two variables different. You should use the base case when accessing the respective variables; otherwise, you will do it wrongly. This sounds awkward, but that is how it happens in C++.

Consider the variable definition given below:

int 2person;

The above is not a valid variable name as the name of the variable, that is, 2person, begins with a number. We said that a variable name should begin either with an underscore or a letter, otherwise, you will get an error. That is very simple! I hope it has "sunk" well! Good!

Multiple variables can also be declared on a single line. The following are some of the valid variable definitions in C++:

int   x, y, z;

char   c, ch;

float j, salary;

double d;

The first line in the above example instructs the C++ compiler to create three variables, namely x, y and z and all of these are of an integer data type.

It is also possible for us to initialize variables while declaring them. To do this, we adhere to the following syntax:

type variable_name = value;

The following examples demonstrate how this can be done:

extern int i = 4, j = 7;   // definition of i and j.

int i = 4, j = 7;   // definition and initializing i and j.

byte z = 20;   // definition and initializes z.

char y = 'y';   // the variable y has the value 'y'.

What we have done in the above examples is that we have declared the variables, reserving memory location for each, and then a value has been stored in that memory location. Woow! That is now amazing! I am sure you are now falling in love with C++!

Loop Types in C++

In some cases, you may have a particular piece of code which you may need to execute it repeatedly or for a specified number of times. The execution of such statements is usually done sequentially.

Programming languages provide us with constructs which help us execute statements with complicated execution paths. This may sound complex for now, but you will realize simple it is in our next section.

The "while" loop

This statement relies on a condition, and the loop will be executed as long as the condition value is found to be true after evaluation. If the condition is found to be false, then the loop will not be executed. The loop takes the following syntax:

while(condition)

```
{

 statement(s);

}
```

In this case, the statement can be single, or we may have multiple statements. Let us demonstrate this by use of an example:

```
#include <iostream>
using namespace std;
 int main ()
{
  // declaring the local variable:
  int x = 5;
  // execution of the while loop
  while( x < 10 )
  {
    cout << "The value of variable x is: " << x << endl;

    x++;

  }
```

```
    return 0;

}
```

Just write the program your text editor and save it with a .cpp extension. Create an executable file from the command line and then execute it. Use the commands we used in our "Hello world" program! Test your power to remember!

You should see the following output on the console:

```
The value of variable x is: 5
The value of variable x is: 6
The value of variable x is: 7
The value of variable x is: 8
The value of variable x is: 9
```

Woow! The output looks amazing! But what did we do. We initialized our variable x to 5. In the statement "while(x<10)", we are setting the loop condition, which is that the value of variable x has to be less than 10. Once the C++ compiler finds itself violating this condition, it will stop its execution. I am sure you are asking yourself, "does the C++ compiler think?" No, it doesn't think. It follows the instructions you give it, and that is what we call computer programming. Awesome! You are now a computer programmer!

Once the loop is executed for the first time, the value of x will be 5, and that is the source of the first line in the above output. It will then proceed and execute the command "x++", which instructs it to increment the value of x by 1. On evaluating the loop for the second time, the value of 6 will be 6, which is less than 10, and the condition will have been satisfied. This explains the source of the second line in the above output. This will continue, but once the loop evaluates and finds that the value of x is 10, the condition (x<10) will be violated, and this will call for termination for execution of the program. That is too sweet, you must be happy about the program!

The "for" Loop

This type of loop is used when you are aware of the number of times that your loop should be executed. It takes the following syntax:

for (init; condition; increment)

{

  statement(s);

}

The "init" is for initialization, and it denotes the initial value of the loop variable. The "condition" specifies the condition which should not be violated. This is where you should specify the maximum number of times that the loop should be executed. The "increment" specifies how the initial value should be incremented to the final value. This can also be a decrement.

Let us use a program to make this easy for you to understand:

```cpp
#include <iostream>
using namespace std;

int main ()
{
    // execution of for loop
    for( int x = 0; x < 10; x = x + 1 )
    {
        cout << "The value of x is: " << x << endl;
    }
    return 0;
}
```

Just write the program in your text editor and give it a name with a ".cpp" extension. After that, run it and you will get the following result:

```
The value of x is: 0
The value of x is: 1
The value of x is: 2
The value of x is: 3
The value of x is: 4
The value of x is: 5
The value of x is: 6
The value of x is: 7
The value of x is: 8
The value of x is: 9
```

In the loop statement, we used the statement "int x=0;", which means that we have initialized the value of variable x to be 0 at first. This explains the source of the first line in the above output. The condition "x<10" signifies that 10 will not be part of the output. The "x=x+1" conditions specifies that the value of the variable x should be incremented by 1 after each execution. You now understand the source of the above output and why the value of x ranges between 0 and 9. If we wanted

10 to be part of the output, then we would have used the condition "x<=10" in the loop statement. That sounds awesome! You can go ahead and try it and observe the output!

Decision Making Statements in C++

These types of statements expect you as the programmer to set multiple conditions together with the statements which will be executed whenever each of the respective condition is met.

Let us discuss some of these decision making statements in C++.

The "if" Statements

This is made up of a Boolean expression, and then some statements. Below is the syntax for the "if" statement in C++:

if(boolean_expression)

```
{

//statement(s) to be executed once the boolean
expression evaluates to true

}
```

Consider the following example:

```
#include <iostream>

using namespace std;

 int main ()

{

  // declaration of local variable:

  int x = 5;

  // checking the boolean condition

  if( x < 10 )

  {

    // if the condition is found to be true, print the
following

    cout << "x is less than 10;" << endl;
```

```
}
    cout << "The value of x is : " << x << endl;


    return 0;
}
```

Again, write the program in a text editor and save it with a .cpp extension in the file name. Compile and execute the program, and you will get the following result:

```
x is less than 10;
The value of x is : 5
```

The "if...else" statement

This is made up of an "if" statement and "else" statement which will be executed in case the Boolean expression evaluates to a false.

This statement takes the following syntax:

if(boolean_expression)

{

   // statement(s) to be executed when the boolean expression is true

}

else

{

   // statement(s) to be executed when the boolean expression is false

}

If the "Boolean_expresion" evaluates to a true, then the statements under it will be executed. If it evaluates to a false, then the statements under the "else" part will be executed.

Consider the following example:

#include <iostream>

```cpp
using namespace std;

int main ()
{
  // declaration of the local variable:
  int x = 50;

  // check for the boolean condition
  if( x < 5 )
  {
    // if condition evaluates to true, print the following
    cout << "x is less than 5;" << endl;
  }
  else
  {
    // if condition evaluates to false, print the following
    cout << "x is not less than 5;" << endl;
  }
  cout << "The value of x is : " << x << endl;
```

return 0;

}

Write and run the above program as usual. You will get the following result:

```
x is not less than 5;
The value of x is : 50
```

We began by setting the value of variable x to be 50. In the "if" statement, we are testing to check to see if the value of the variable is less than 5, which is not true. This means that "if(x<5)" condition will evaluate to a false, and the statements within its block ({}) will be skipped.

The C++ compiler will then skip to the "else" part which is the default, and its statements will be executed. This explains the source of the output.

"if...else if...else" Statement

We can choose to add an "else if...else" statement to an "if" statement so that we can be able to test the various conditions. This done using the following syntax:

```
if(boolean_expression 1)

{

   // Will be executed once the boolean expression 1
   evaluates to true

}

else if( boolean_expression 2)

{

   // Will be executed once the boolean expression 2
   evaluates to true

}

else if( boolean_expression 3)

{

   // Exec Will be executed once the boolean
   expression 3 evaluates to true

}
```

else

{

// will be executed if none of the above conditions is found to be true

}

The following example demonstrates how this can be done:

```cpp
#include <iostream>

using namespace std;
 int main ()
{
  // declaration of the local variable:
  int x = 50;
   // checking the boolean condition
  if( x == 40 )
  {
    // if the condition evaluates to true, print the following
    cout << "The value of x is 40" << endl;
  }
```

```cpp
   else if( x == 30 )

   {

      // if else if condition evaluates to true

      cout << "The value of x is 30" << endl;

   }

   else if( x == 20 )

   {

      // if else if condition evaluates to true

      cout << "The value of x is 20" << endl;

   }

   else

   {

      // if none of your conditions evaluates to true

      cout << "The value of x did not match any
condition" << endl;
   }

   cout << "The exact value of x is : " << x << endl;


   return 0;

}
```

Once you execute the above program, you will get the following result:

```
The value of x did not match any condition
The exact value of x is : 50
```

The value of variable x was first set to 50. In all our test conditions using the "if" and the "else if" statements, none of the used values matches the true value of x, and this means that their statements will not be executed. The C++ compiler will execute the default "else" part at the last part of the program, and this explains the source of the above output. Now that it is easy for you to use decision making statements in C++. That is how easy it is!

Chapter 2- Java

Java is simply a high-level programming language which was initially developed by the Suns Microsystems and then released in the year 1995. Java is a versatile programming language as you can create standard, distributed applications as well as applications to be embedded on the web using it.

Before getting started to program in Java, we should first setup the environment. There are free environment for your use online. However, it is good for you to learn how to set it up locally on your machine.

The SE (Standard Edition) is available for your free download from the Oracle website. Look for Java runtime environment (JRE) or the Java Development Toolkit (JDK) from the website and then download it. Once the download is complete, double click on the executable file so as to begin the installation process.

Path Setup

Once the JRE or JDK has been installed, there is a need for us to set the path variable. After installation of the above, the path should be set to the directory "*c:\Program Files\java\jdk*".

In Windows, this can be done as follows:

Navigate to the directory "*c:\Program Files\java\jdk\bin*" and copy the path. Right click "My Computer", then choose "Properties". Click the button for "Environment variables" found below the "Advanced" tab. Identify the "Path" parameter, click on it, and then choose "Edit. Add the path you have copied, ensuring that you add a semicolon at the end.

For Linux users, the path has to be set to where the installation of binaries was done.

Once the path has been setup, you should ensure that you have the text editor of choice. Some of the common text editors include Notepad in Windows, Netbeans and Eclipse.

The Hello world Example

Open your text editor and then type the following java program:

```
public class HelloWorld{

public static void main(String args[]){

        System.out.println("Hello world");

    }

}
```

Once you are done with typing the program, save it with the name "HelloWorld.java" if you were doing it a text editor such as Notepad. Note that the file name has to match the name of the class. Woow! What is a class? Do not worry; we are to discuss this in the next section. Now you can open your terminal and then navigate to the directory in which you have saved the file.

You should then compile program to check for errors and create an executable file, which is the .class file. This can be done by typing the following command:

javac HelloWorld.java

The command should be typed exactly as above. Ooh! Java is case sensitive. Ensure that the name of the file is types as shown above, with uppercase "H" and Uppercase "W". The rest should be lowercase. You can then hit the enter key. You will be shown whether the program has errors or not. In our case, it should have no errors. The command will create a file named "HelloWorld.class", and this is the executable object. To execute this, run the following command on the command line:

java HelloWorld.class

You should see the text "Hello world" printed on the terminal.

For those who are using Netbeans as the text editor, right click within the file and then click on "Run file". You should see the following output:

Hello world

Java Data Types and Variables

A java variable represents a name for a memory location. Java supports three types of variables namely local, instance and the static variables.

Consider the following example:

int age=10;

In the above example, age is a variable. Let us discuss the types of variables briefly:

1. Local variable- this is a variable declared within a method and it is only accessible within that method.

2. Instance variable- a variable which has been declared inside a class and out the method.

3. Static variable- this is a variable which has

4. Declared to be static.

The following example demonstrates how these three types of variables can be declared in Java:

class A{

int age=10;//instance variable

```
static int j=50;//static variable

void method(){

double height=29.76;//local variable

}

}//end of class
```

The variable "age" has been declared immediately after the class and it is not inside any method. In Java, a method is named with () at the end. This is an instance variable. The variable j has been declared with a static keyword, making it a static variable. The variable "height" has been declared inside the method(), and it will only be accessible within the block ({}) of this method.

It is possible for us to access the value of a variable. The following example demonstrates how this can be done:

public class VarExample {

```java
public static void main(String []args) {

  int m=10;

  System.out.println("The value of m is:\t"+ m);

 }
}
```

Once you compile and run the above program, it will give you the following result:

```
The value of m is:        10
```

The value of the variable was accessed in the line "System.out.println("The value of m is:\t"+ m);"

Java Operators

Operators are the mathematical symbols which can be used for doing arithmetic operations. The following is an example which shows how you can perform arithmetic or mathematical operations in a program, other than using a calculator. I am sure this sounds funny, but you will get to appreciate it shortly. Here is the example:

```
public class MyClass {

    public static void main(String args[]) {
        int w = 2;
        int x = 10;
        int y = 4;
        int z = 8;
        System.out.println("w + x = " + (w + x) );
        System.out.println("w - x = " + (w - x) );
        System.out.println("w * x = " + (w * x) );
        System.out.println("x / w = " + (x / w) );
        System.out.println("x % w = " + (x % w) );
        System.out.println("y % w = " + (y % w) );
        System.out.println("w++  = " + (w++) );
        System.out.println("x--  = " + (w--) );
```

```
// Check the difference between these

System.out.println("z++  = " + (z++) );

System.out.println("++z  = " + (++z) );
  }
}
```

Just write the program in a text editor and then run it. You will observe the following as the output:

```
w + x = 12
w - x = -8
w * x = 20
x / w = 5
x % w = 0
y % w = 0
w++     = 2
x--     = 3
z++     = 8
++z     = 10
```

The only operator which might be a bit complex to you is the modulus operator (%). This returns the remainder after division.

int w = 2;

   int x = 10;

int y = 4;

The "x(10)%w(2)" gives 0 since 10 divide by 2 is 5, with no remainder. The "y(4)%w(2)" gives 0 since 2 gocs into 4 2 times, and no remainder. Let me explain this one further.

Suppose you have 10%3, the answer will be 1. 10 divide by 3 is 3, with a remainder of 1 (10-9). That is it! As simple as that! Feel happy!

Decision Making in Java

Java supports the use of decision making statements. This means that you are able to implement the logic for making decisions in you Java program. This sounds sweet!

In looping, we are able to control the number of times that a statement of statements will be executed. Let us discuss some of the decision making statements supported in java.

The "if" Statement

The "if" statement tests some specified condition. If it evaluates to true, its corresponding statements will be executed. It takes the syntax given below:

if(condition){

//the code which will be executed

}

Consider the following example which demonstrates how this statement can be used:

public class IfStatementExample {

public static void main(String[] args) {

  int age=10;

  if(age>5){

System.out.print("Your age is more than 5");

```
  }

}

}
```

Write the program and then execute it. You will get the result given below:

```
Your age is more than 5
```

The value of age was set to 10. In our test condition, we are checking whether this value is greater than 5, which is true. The condition evaluates to true, and the corresponding statement was executed giving us the above output. If the condition was false, then we would get no result.

The "if...else" statement

This evaluates a condition in the "if" part. If this is true, the statement under the "if" will be executed, otherwise, the statements under the "else" part will be executed. It takes the syntax given below:

if(condition){

//code to be executed if the condition is true

}else{

//code to execute if the condition is false

}

Consider the example given below:

public class IfElseStatement {

public static void main(String[] args) {

```java
int num=15;

if(num%2==0){

        System.out.println("It is an
    even number");

      }else{

        System.out.println("It is an odd number");

      }

  }

  }
```

Execute the program and you will get the following result:

```
It is an odd number
```

The value of num is 15. If you divide this by 2, you get 7 and a remainder of 1. The 1 which is a remainder is not equal to 0, hence our "if" condition will evaluate to false. This will lead to execution of the "else" part.

The "if...else...if" Statement

In this statement, we evaluate multiple statements. It takes the syntax given below:

if(condition1){

//code to execute if the condition1 is true

}else if(condition2){

//code to execute if the condition2 is true

}

else if(condition3){

//code to execute if the condition3 is true

}

...

else{

//code to execute if all conditions are false

}

Consider the example given below:

```
public class IfElseIfStatement {

public static void main(String[] args) {

    int marks=58;


    if(marks<40){

        System.out.println("You have failed the exam");

    }
```

```java
    else if(marks>=40 && marks<50){

        System.out.println("Your grade is D");

    }

    else if(marks>=50 && marks<60){

        System.out.println("Your grade is C");

    }

    else if(marks>=60 && marks<70){

        System.out.println("Your grade is B");

    }

    else if(marks>=70){

        System.out.println("Your grade is A");

    }else{

        System.out.println("Your marks are
invalid!Kindly double check");

    }
```

```
}

}
```

Write and run the program. You will get the result given below:

Your grade is C

The value of marks was set to 58. These marks lies between 50 and 60, hence the condition "if marks>=50&&<60" will evaluate to true, and its corresponding statement will be executed. This explains the source of the output. You can try to change the marks and observe the result that you get. However, ensure that you enter valid marks, ranging between 0 and 100. If you put a negative number or any non-number value, then you will get the result that the marks are invalid. This is because the "else" part of the program will be executed.

Java "switch" Statement

This statement is used when we need to execute a single statement from multiple conditions which we have. It takes the following syntax:

```
switch(expression){

case value1:

 //code to execute;

 break; //optional

case value2:

 //code to execute;

 break; //optional

......


default:
```

//the code to execute in case all cases are false;

}

Consider the example given below:

```java
public class SwitchStatement {

public static void main(String[] args) {

  int age=40;

  switch(age){

  case 20: System.out.println("Your      age      is
20");break;

  case 30: System.out.println("Your      age      is
30");break;

  case 40: System.out.println("Your      age      is
40");break;

  default:System.out.println("The   age   was   not
matched!");
```

```
    }

}

}
```

Write the program and run it. It will determine the value for

your variable "age". It should give you the following result:

Your age is 40

I am sure you understand the source of the above output. We

set the value for the "age" variable to be 40. The Java compiler

will match the condition for "case: 40", and its statement will

be executed. The rest of the case statements will be ignored.

The "break" statement should be used at the end of each case

statement so as it to prevent it from preceding its execution to the next case statement. That is how simple the "switch" statement is!

Java Loops

In looping, we are able to control the number of times that a statement of statements will be executed. Let us discuss some of the loop statements supported in java.

The "for" Loop

This loop is used when we need to execute a statement or statements repeatedly. A simple for loop statement takes the following syntax:

for(initialization;condition;increment/decrement){

//code to execute

}

Consider the example given below:

```
public class ForStatement {

public static void main(String[] args) {

    for(int j=0;j<10;j++){

        System.out.println("The value of j is"+ j);

    }

}

}
```

Just write the program and run it. You will get the following result:

```
The value of j is0
The value of j is1
The value of j is2
The value of j is3
The value of j is4
The value of j is5
The value of j is6
The value of j is7
The value of j is8
The value of j is9
```

The value of j ranges between 0 and 9. This is because it has to be less than 10, meaning that 10 is not part of the output. Whenever the Java compiler finds itself violating this condition, it will halt execution, and this explains the source of the above output.

The "for...each" Loop

This type of loop is used when we need to traverse a collection or an array. In this loop, no increment is needed, making it easy for us to use it. In this case, the elements are accessed by use of the respective indices. This statement takes the following syntax:

```
for(Type var:array){

//code to execute

}
```

Consider the following example:

```
public class ForEachStatement {
public static void main(String[] args) {
   int array[]={10,20,30 ,40,50};
   for(int k:array){
     System.out.println("The value of k is"+k);
   }
 }
}
```

Write the program and then run it. You will get the following result:

```
The value of k is10
The value of k is20
The value of k is30
The value of k is40
The value of k is50
```

The integer "k" has been declared to access the values of the array. Access to array values is done by use of colon (:) operator as shown in the above example.

The "while" Loop

This is the best loop if you are not sure of the number of times to iterate your statements. The loop takes the following syntax:

```java
while(condition){

//code to execute

}
```

Consider the example given below:

```java
public class WhileStatement {
public static void main(String[] args) {
    int k=0;
    while(k<10){
        System.out.println("The value of K is:"+k);
    k++;
    }
}
}
```

Write and run the program, and it will give you the following result:

```
The value of K is:0
The value of K is:1
The value of K is:2
The value of K is:3
The value of K is:4
The value of K is:5
The value of K is:6
The value of K is:7
The value of K is:8
The value of K is:9
```

We have used the condition "while(k<10)", meaning that the value of k should be less than 10, and the 10 is not included. The initial value for the variable "k" is 0. This is why the loop iterates between 0 and 9. That is simple!

Chapter 3- Python

Object is a high-level; object oriented and interpreted programming language. For you to program in Python, you have to setup the environment first. For those use current Linux distributions, the Python interpreter comes installed. You can check for it at the terminal by typing the following command "python". If it is installed, the version will be displayed.

If it is not installed, then you have to download the binary installables for Python. Ensure that you download the correct one based on the operating system that you are using.

If you are using a Linux distribution, install Python by running the following command on the terminal:

$sudo apt-get install python3-minimal

For the case of Windows users, it easy on your part as you just have to download and double click on the executable file, and the installation process will be launched. Once the installation process is complete, open the terminal and set the path using the command:

path %path%;C:\Python

You will then have setup the path variable in your machine.

The Hello word Example

Now that your environment is ready for programming, you can go ahead to write your first program. Just open the Python terminal or command line and then type the following on it. If you on Linux, type "python" on the Linux terminal and it will be opened:

>>> print ("Hello world")

You can then hit the "Enter" key and you will see the text "Hello world" printed on the terminal.

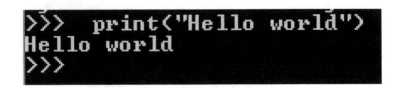

That way, the code was written on the terminal, and this is referred to as interactive programming mode. In the scripting mode, the code is written in a file, which is saved with a ".py" extension.

Just open a text editor and then type the above code in it. Save the file as "hello.py". The .py extension signifies that we have created a Python file.

After that, you can run the program. I n Linux, open your terminal and type the following command:

$ python hello.py

On Windows, ensure that you are currently on the directory where you have installed the Python. You can then type the command as follows:

C:\Python34>Python hello.py

Variables

Variables are used for the purpose of reserving some memory location.

The declaration of a variable in Python happens automatically after assigning a value to it. The assignment is done by use of the equal(=) sign. Consider the example given below:

name = "Mercy"   # String assignment

age = 10   # Integer assignment

height   = 10.8   # Floating point assignment

print (name)

print (age)

print (height)

The program should give the following result after running it:

```
Mercy
10
10.8
```

It is also possible for you to assign a single value that you have to the several variables, at this will be done simultaneously. The following example shows you how to do it:

p = q = r = 100

In the above example, we have created an integer object of 100, and our three variables, that is, p, q and r have been assigned to that object. This means that each of these variables will have a value of 100.

It is also possible for you to assign the multiple objects that you have to multiple variables. The following example demonstrates this:

p, q, r = 10, 20, "mercy"

I am sure that sounds amazing to you! You must begin to love Python.

Basic Operators

It is possible for us to perform some mathematical calculations in Python. In this case, we will be having two operands and an operator. The operands are the values which we will manipulate, whereas the operator is the symbol which will define the kind of mathematical operations we should perform. Consider the following example:

7 * 4 = 28

In the above example, 7 and 8 are the operands, while the *
symbol is the operator which shows that we are going to
perform a multiplication operation.

Let us give a simple example which shows how we can use
arithmetic operators in Python:

p = 31

q = 5

r = 0

r = p + q

print ("The value of r is: ", r)

r = p - q

print ("The value of r is: ", r)

r = p * q

print ("The value of r is: ", r)

```
r = p / q

print ("The value of r is: ", r)


r = p % q

print ("The value of r is: ", r)


p = 2

q = 3

r = p**q

print ("The value of r is: ", r)


p = 10

q = 5

r = p//q

print ("The value of r is: ", r)
```

Once you run the program, you will get the following result:

```
The value of r is:   36
The value of r is:   26
The value of r is:   155
The value of r is:   6.2
The value of r is:   1
The value of r is:   8
The value of r is:   2
```

Most of the above arithmetic operators are very common to you, but some are new. The % is the modulus operator, and it gives the remainder after division. In our case we are dividing 31 by 5, and the remainder is 1. Why? 31 divide by 6 is 5, which gives 30, remaining with 1. Very Simple!

Decision Making

Have you wished to write Python statements capable of "thinking"? Let us guide you on how to do this by use of decision making statements.

The "if" statement

This is made up of a Boolean expression which is then followed by one or more statements. Its syntax is simple as shown below:

if expression:

  statement(s)

The Python interpreter evaluates the expression, and if it finds it to be true, the block of statements below it will be executed.

Consider the basic example given below:

age = 24

if age:

  print ("Your age is:")

  print (age)

height = 20

```python
if height:

   print ("Your height is:")

   print (height)

print ("That is good!")
```

In the above example, we have two variables, that is, age and height. Each has its own value. We just wanted to check whether those are the variables we have and then print their values. That is what we have done! Very basic!

The Python "if...else" statement

This statement involves creating an "if" statement together with an optional "else" part which will be executed in case the "if" Boolean expression evaluates to a false. This is the syntax for this statement:

```python
if expression:

   statement(s)

else:

   statement(s)
```

In case the expression is false, the statements below the "else" statement will be executed.

Consider the following example:

age=10

if age<10:

   print ("You are too young")

else:

   print ("You have grown up")

   print ("I wish all the best in your life")

Once you run the above program, you will get the following result:

```
You have grown up
I wish all the best in your life
```

If the age was set to a value which is less than 10, we will have the following:

```
age=8
if age<10:

    print ("You are too young")
else:
    print ("You have grown up")
    print ("I wish all the best in your life")
```

Once you run the above program, you will get the result shown below:

```
You are too young
```

In the first program, we set the value of age to 10. The condition "if age<10" means that whether the value of variable age is less than 10. If it is true, then the statement which is below will be executed. In the first example, the condition was false since the value of age is 10, which is not less than 10. This makes the statements below the "else" part to be executed. In the second example, the condition "if age<10" was met since the value of age is 8, which is less than 10. This is why the statement below the "if" statement was executed. You have to pay attention to indentation; otherwise, you will get an error or an undesired output. That is how Python works.

Nested "if" Statements

In some cases, you may need to perform another check once the first one evaluates to true. This is the best scenario for you to use nested "if" statement. This takes the following syntax:

if expression1:

   statement(s)

   if expression2:

     statement(s)

   elif expression3:

statement(s)

else

statement(s)

elif expression4:

statement(s)

else:

statement(s)

Consider the example given below:

```
var=10
if var%2==0:
   if var%5==0:
      print ("Divisible by 2 and 5")
   else:
      print ("divisible by 2 not divisible by 5")
else:
   if var%3==0:
      print ("divisible by 3 not divisible by 2")
   else:
```

print ("not Divisible by 2 not divisible by 3")

Execute the program and you get the following result:

`Divisible by 2 and 5`

In the program, it checks for the condition "if var%2==0", and this evaluates to true. This is because when 10 is divided by 2, the remainder is 0. This statement evaluates to true, but has a nested "if" statements, so the Python interpreter will proceed to evaluate the nested "if", which is "if var%5==0". This also evaluates to true as 10 divided by 5 gives 0 as the remainder. The statement below these two conditions was executed, explaining the source of the output. The execution of the program halts there.

Let us alter the program a bit and see what will happen.

What if we alter the program to the following?

```
var=11
if var%2==0:
  if var%5==0:
    print ("Divisible by 2 and 5")
  else:
    print ("divisible by 2 not divisible by 5")
else:
  if var%3==0:
    print ("divisible by 3 not divisible by 2")
  else:
    print  ("not Divisible by 2 not divisible by 3")
```

We have set the value of var to 11. This is neither divisible by 2, 3 nor by 5. The program gives the following result after execution:

```
not Divisible by 2 not divisible by 3
```

If we alter the value of var to a number which is divisible by 3 only, we will have the following:

```
var=21
if var%2==0:
   if var%5==0:
     print ("Divisible by 2 and 5")
   else:
     print ("divisible by 2 not divisible by 5")
else:
   if var%3==0:
     print ("divisible by 3 not divisible by 2")
   else:
     print  ("not Divisible by 2 not divisible by 3")
```

The program will give the following result:

```
divisible by 3 not divisible by 2
```

Woow! That is fantastic! That is how you can instruct the Python interpreter to think.

Looping

With loops in Python, you can specify the number of times that you need a block of statements to be executed. Let us discuss some of the basic loops in Python:

The "while" Loop

With this type of loop, you have to set a condition, and the loop will continue running as long as this condition is true. If the condition becomes false, then the loop will no longer be executed.

The statement takes the following syntax:

while expression:

   statement(s)

Consider the example given below:

```
age = 10
while (age < 18):
    print ('You are a minor')
    age = age + 1


print ("You are now a grown up!")
```

The program will give you the following result after execution:

```
You are a minor
You are a minor
You are a minor
You are a minor
You are a minor
You are a minor
You are a minor
You are a minor
You are now a grown up!
```

The initial value of age is 10. The condition "while(age < 18)" states that as long the value of age is less than 18, then the statement "you are a minor" will be shown. However, if the value of age gets to 18, you are no longer a minor, meaning that the "while" condition is about to be violated, forcing the interpreter to execute the statement outside the loop.

If the value of age was set to a value 18 or higher, then the final statement will be executed.

```
age = 20

while (age < 18):

    print ('You are a minor')

    age = age + 1


print ("You are now a grown up!")
```

The result will be as follows:

```
You are now a grown up!
```

The "for" Loop

Use this statement when you are aware of the number of times that you need to execute your loop. It takes the syntax given below:

for iterating_var in sequence:

   statements(s)

A simple "for" loop program can be written as follows:

for num in list(range(10)):

   print (num)

This will give you the following result:

0

1

2

3

4

5

6

7

8

9

Conclusion

We have come to the end of this book. You should now be aware of how to write basic programs in C++, Java and Python. These languages are object-oriented, meaning that we can implement object-oriented features in them. Examples of such features include the use of classes and objects. These three languages are very popular in the market, which means that you should be aware of how to code in them!